STICKMEN'S GUIDE TO EARTH'S ATMOSPHERE
IN LAYERS

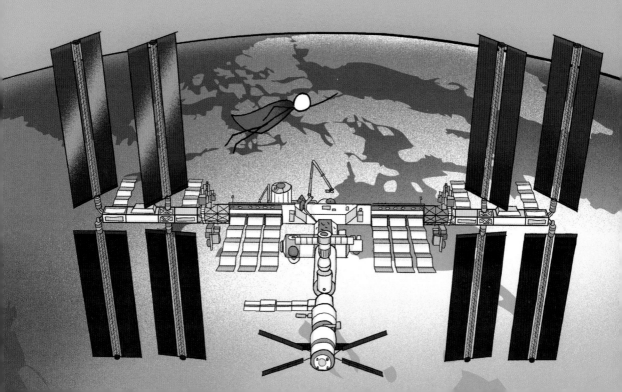

Thanks to the creative team:
Senior Editor: Alice Peebles
Consultant: Jacqueline Mitton
Fact checking: Kate Mitchell
Design: www.collaborate.agency

Hungry Tomato™
A division of Lerner Publishing Group, Inc.
241 First Avenue North
Minneapolis, MN 55401 USA

For reading levels and more information, look up this title at www.lernerbooks.com.

Main body text set in Avenir Next Medium 9.5/12. Typeface provided by Linotype AG.

Library of Congress Cataloging-in-Publication Data

The Cataloging-in-Publication Data for *Stickmen's Guide to Earth's Atmosphere in Layers* is on file at the Library of Congress.
ISBN 978-1-5124-0617-7 (lib. bdg.)
ISBN 978-1-5124-1181-2 (pbk.)
ISBN 978-1-5124-0931-4 (EB pdf)

Manufactured in the United States of America
1 - VP - 7/15/16

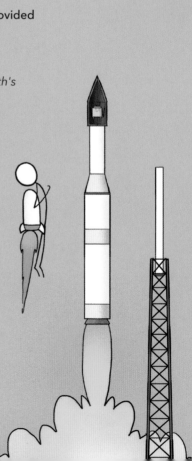

STICKMEN'S GUIDE TO EARTH'S ATMOSPHERE
IN LAYERS

by Catherine Chambers
Illustrated by John Paul de Quay

HUNGRY TOMATO.

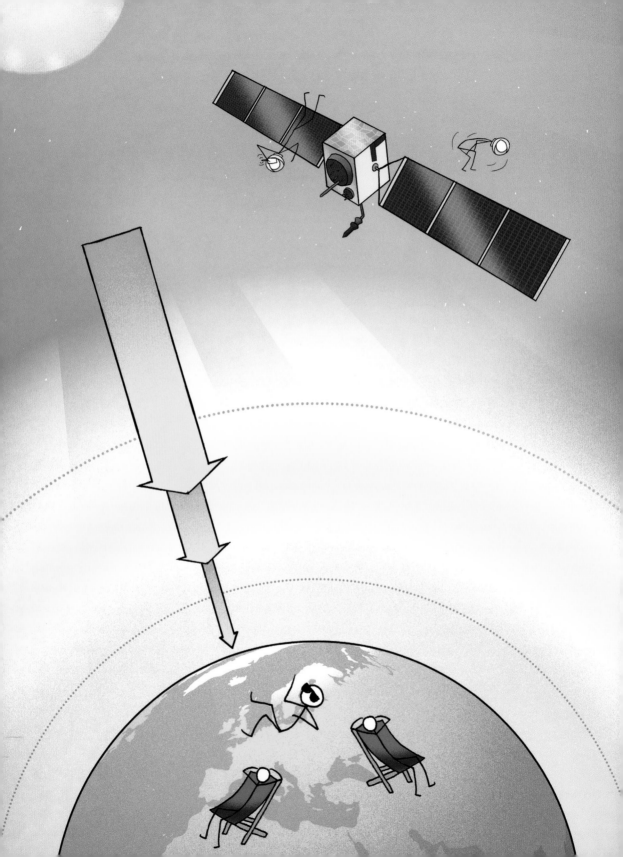

Contents

The Atmosphere

When we look up at the sky, we are looking through layers of gases called the atmosphere. These layers wrap around Earth like a pile of blankets, some thick and others thin. Each layer is made of a mixture of gases, covers a range of temperatures and air pressure, and has a different effect on the way we live on Earth.

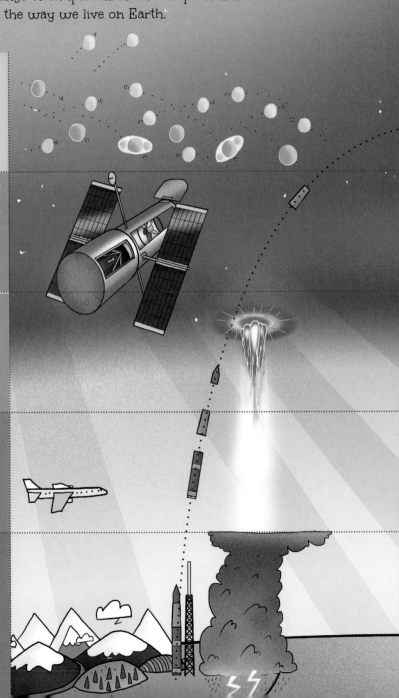

Exosphere

From around 375 miles (600 kilometers)

Pressure is extremely low, gases are very thin and some escape into space. Most satellites orbit Earth here.

Thermosphere

Around 53-375 miles (85-600 km)

Gases are still thin, pressure is very low and the temperatures increase with height. Bright colored lights pulsate.

Mesosphere

Around 30-53 miles (50-85 km)

Temperatures are very cold. Meteors shoot through and burn up. The highest clouds put on a light show over the poles.

Stratosphere

Ranging from 4-30 miles (6-50 km)

The tips of Earth's highest clouds reach here. A layer of ozone gases protects Earth from the Sun's harmful rays.

Troposphere

Ranging from 0-12 miles (0-20 km)

In this layer, we can breathe oxygen and plants use carbon dioxide to grow. The boundary with the stratosphere varies.

High in the Exosphere

This layer of very thin gases begins around 375 miles (600 km) above Earth's surface. Is it part of Earth's atmosphere? Or is it part of outer space? Scientists cannot agree! But a lot happens here.

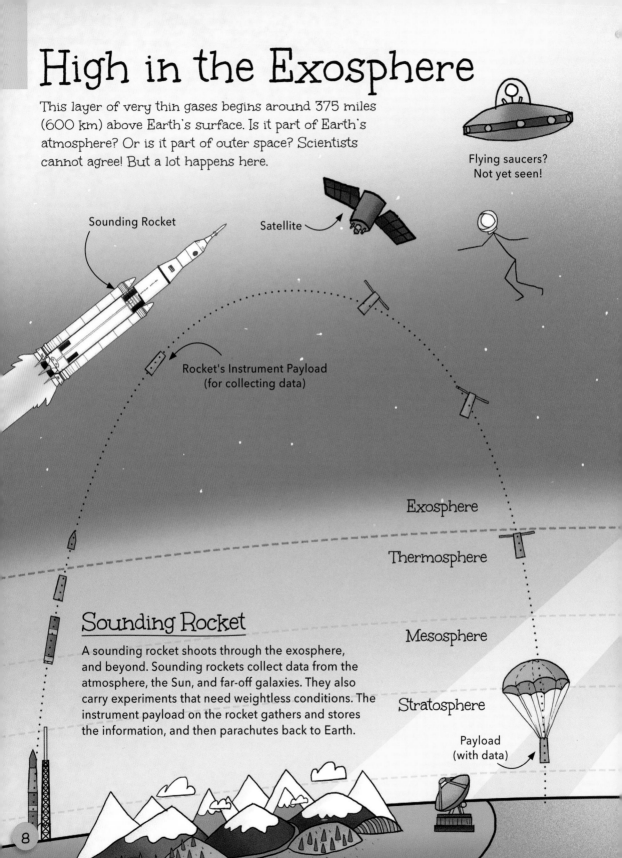

Flying saucers? Not yet seen!

Sounding Rocket

Satellite

Rocket's Instrument Payload (for collecting data)

Exosphere

Thermosphere

Mesosphere

Sounding Rocket

A sounding rocket shoots through the exosphere, and beyond. Sounding rockets collect data from the atmosphere, the Sun, and far-off galaxies. They also carry experiments that need weightless conditions. The instrument payload on the rocket gathers and stores the information, and then parachutes back to Earth.

Stratosphere

Payload (with data)

Power of the Sun

The Sun is a very active searing-hot star that radiates energy toward Earth. At times, the Sun emits strong blasts of ultraviolet (UV) rays (found beyond the violet end of the light spectrum), as shown here, and X-rays. These make the thermosphere below bulge up into the exosphere. The boundary between these layers is never exact, but it is more stable at some times than others.

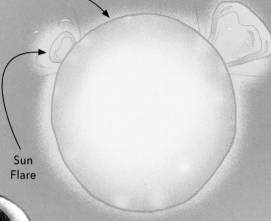

Sun Flare

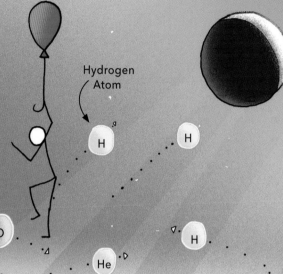

Hydrogen Atom

On the Way to the Moon

The upper edge of the exosphere marks the end of Earth's atmosphere and the beginning of space. It is also halfway to the Moon.

Helium Atom

Carbon Dioxide Molecule

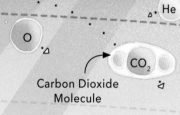

Oxygen Atom

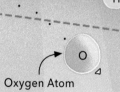

Glowing Exosphere

Pictures of Earth taken with a UV telescope show the exosphere glowing. This eerie light is called the geocorona. It is created by the Sun's UV rays reflecting off the cloud of hydrogen atoms surrounding Earth.

Speedy Gases

The exosphere's gases are mainly hydrogen atoms, with some helium and carbon dioxide. There are some oxygen atoms too. These gases speed along curved paths, without colliding. Earth's gravity pulls down most of the gases toward the troposphere, but the fastest zoom off into space.

Troposphere

Satellites in the Exosphere

About two thousand artificial satellites orbit our planet at a height of about 12,400 miles (20,000 km) and above. They relay data, communication signals, or images to Earth through an antennae, and use solar power. They operate in the exosphere where they are safe from atmospheric drag, which would make them spiral down to Earth and burn up.

Satellite Science

Each satellite has its own mission and instruments. Some track the paths of Earth's cyclones and wildfires, or monitor changes in ice sheets and oceans. Other satellites measure gases such as carbon dioxide or ozone that have important effects on our planet. Yet others are telescopes for observing planets, stars, and galaxies far away.

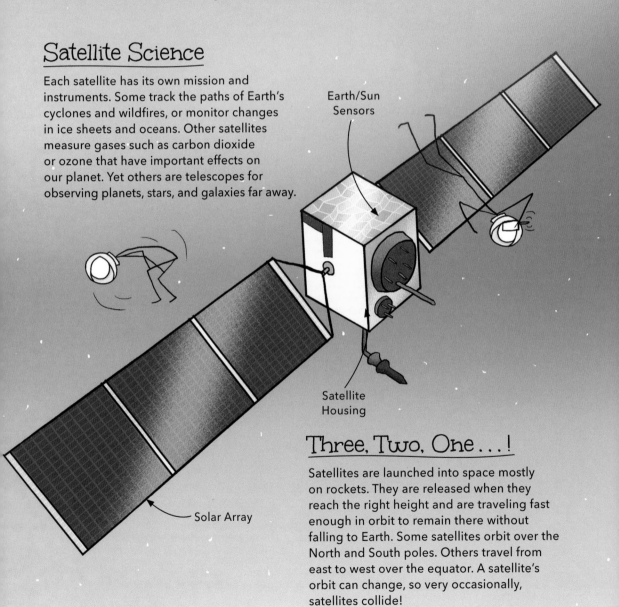

Earth/Sun Sensors

Satellite Housing

Solar Array

Three, Two, One...!

Satellites are launched into space mostly on rockets. They are released when they reach the right height and are traveling fast enough in orbit to remain there without falling to Earth. Some satellites orbit over the North and South poles. Others travel from east to west over the equator. A satellite's orbit can change, so very occasionally, satellites collide!

Orbiting Satellites

The Global Positioning System (GPS) satellites are each in one of six orbits that cover the world. A GPS satellite takes about twelve hours to complete one orbit.

GPS Satellite

Radio Signals with Location and Time Information

GPS Receiver

GPS Rocket

GPS Satellite

Engine

Gantry (for servicing rocket at launchpad)

Booster Core (for powering rocket to higher level)

Engine (for powering rocket at initial stage)

Where Are You?

GPS is a network of about thirty satellites that can pinpoint places on our planet. They beam down radio waves, traveling at the speed of light, that are picked up by receivers on Earth. A receiver calculates its distance from at least four satellites, and then works out its exact location on Earth.

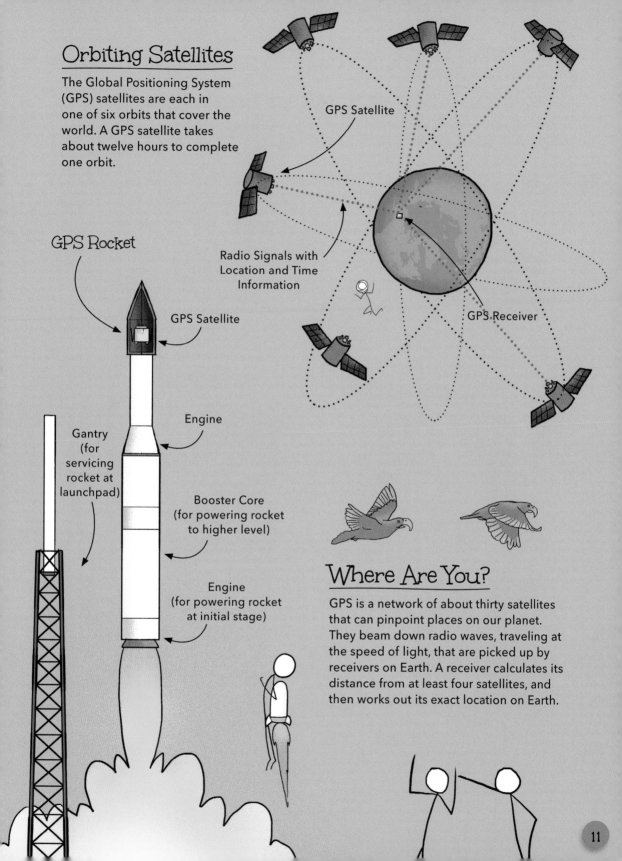

Floating in the Thermosphere

The deep thermosphere layer reaches from around 53 to 375 miles (85 to 600 km) above Earth. Its main gas is nitrogen, with some oxygen, helium, and hydrogen. Toward the base of this layer, temperature falls and gravity's pull is stronger.

Working Together

The International Space Station (ISS) is the largest artificial object ever put in space. It orbits 200 miles (320 km) above Earth, sixteen times each day. A total of fifteen countries cooperated to build ISS, and astronauts from those countries spend months on board, conducting scientific experiments. The weightlessness of space brings scientific results that can be helpful to us on Earth. You can track the ISS in real time online!

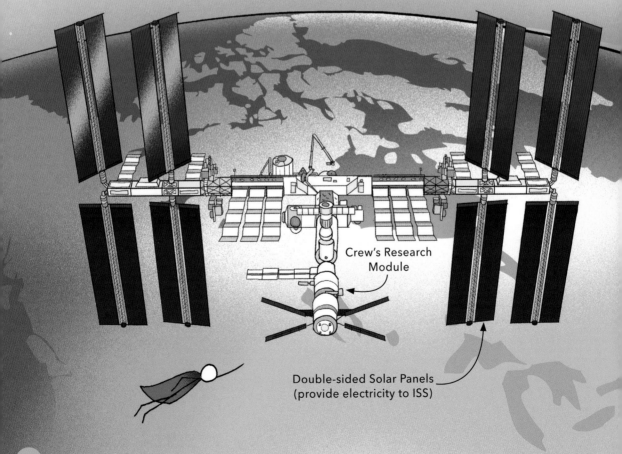

Crew's Research Module

Double-sided Solar Panels (provide electricity to ISS)

Amazing Astronauts

Astronauts are scientists and engineers trained to work inside and outside space vehicles. A space walk lasts between five and eight hours, depending on the astronaut's job. An astronaut is tethered to the spacecraft, to prevent the astronaut from floating away. A backpack with small jet thrusters allows the astronaut to move around in space.

Oxygen Line

Safety Tether

One X-15 rocket plane recorded a flying height of 65 miles (100 km).

X-15 Rocket Plane

This experimental, hypersonic rocket-powered aircraft first flew in 1959 and still holds the speed record for a manned, powered aircraft. It reached 4,520 miles per hour (7,274 kilometers per hour) and Neil Armstrong was one of its pilots.

External Fuel Tank

Super Space Shuttle

The space shuttle, in operation from 1982 to 2011, was the only manned, winged aircraft that could move into orbit and back again, returning its crew and payload. Its robotic arm, the Canadarm, was used to fix the ISS. It also took hold of the Hubble Space Telescope (see page 14) so that repairs could be made.

Two rocket boosters provided 71 percent of the thrust needed for launch.

Orbiter (the only shuttle component that went into orbit)

Looking into Space

The Hubble Space Telescope orbits Earth in the thermosphere at about 340 miles (547 km) above Earth. For more than twenty-five years, it has beamed back spectacular images of space, including planets, comets, exploding stars, nebulae (gas and dust clouds), and galaxies. Scientists use Hubble's data and images to learn more about these objects and the universe.

Through the Telescope

Hubble captures its amazing images using both visible light and radiation we cannot see: ultraviolet and infrared, at either end of the light spectrum. It has five different instruments with cameras for taking particular kinds of images. Some of them can split light into its different wavelengths and some take pictures through special filters.

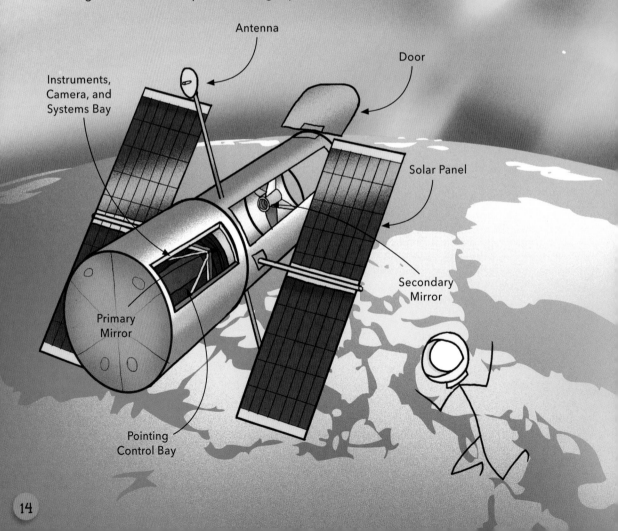

Antenna

Door

Instruments, Camera, and Systems Bay

Solar Panel

Secondary Mirror

Primary Mirror

Pointing Control Bay

Southern Pinwheel

This is Hubble's view of a spiral galaxy in the constellation Hydra, nicknamed the Southern Pinwheel. Lying 15 million light years away, it is relatively near and easier to see than other galaxies. The swirling blues and pinks are glowing gas where stars are being born. Among the thousands of star clusters and individual stars in this galaxy are supernova remnants –traces of giant stars that have exploded and died.

Pictures in the Dark

Hubble has no flash to take images in the darkness of space. Instead, it aims and fixes onto its target with its Pointing Control System, which uses three special instruments called Fine Guidance Sensors. Then its primary mirror captures and concentrates the light from space, reflecting it onto a smaller secondary mirror. This mirror focuses the light onto one of the cameras or instruments.

Bright Lights in the Mesosphere

The mesosphere is a thin layer of mixed gases around 30 to 53 miles (50 to 85 km) above Earth. With fewer air molecules to absorb the sun's radiation, temperatures near the upper mesosphere plunge to –130°F (–90°C), the coldest in our atmosphere. Meteors shoot into this layer and then burn up.

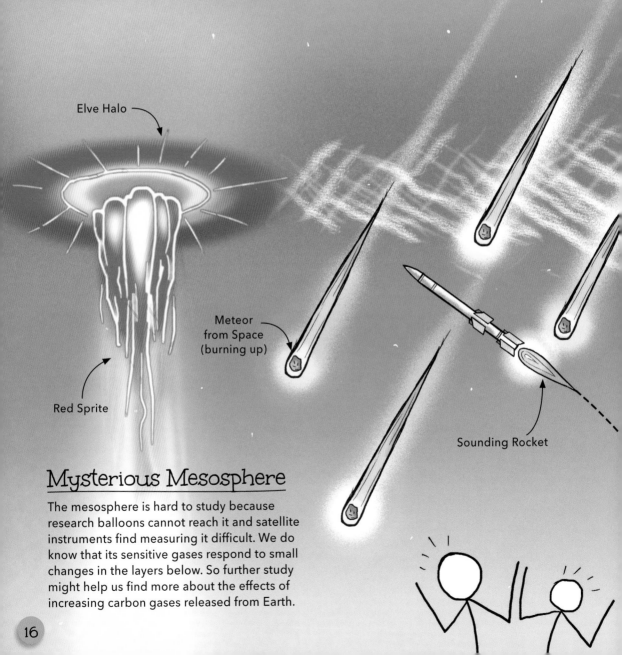

Elve Halo

Meteor from Space (burning up)

Sounding Rocket

Red Sprite

Mysterious Mesosphere

The mesosphere is hard to study because research balloons cannot reach it and satellite instruments find measuring it difficult. We do know that its sensitive gases respond to small changes in the layers below. So further study might help us find more about the effects of increasing carbon gases released from Earth.

Night Clouds

Very high night clouds, known as noctilucent clouds, occasionally illuminate the sky in the mesosphere, near Earth's poles. They are made of ice crystals that scatter light, making them shine. They occur in the freezing upper limit of this layer and are also known as Polar Mesospheric Clouds.

Night Cloud

Lightning Storm

Red Sprites and Elves

Long streaks of faint red light flash briefly above heavy storm clouds and lightning from the troposphere way below. A halo-shaped glow, or elve, forms above it (left). We do not know exactly why they form, but these fascinating lights are captured best by very sensitive, low light level television (LLLTV) equipment.

Airglow

The upper layers of the atmosphere give out very faint light the whole time. This is called airglow. Looking through the atmosphere from space, it makes a glowing band. Airglow is mostly caused by particles and radiation from the Sun affecting gases in the atmosphere in different ways.

Airglow

Stormy Stratosphere

The stratosphere can reach down to around 4 miles (6 km) and rise to its highest point around 30 miles (50 km) above Earth. These boundaries depend on the seasons and where you are in the world. They are also affected by electrical storms in the troposphere below.

Mesosphere

Bright Blue Jets

Blue jets are narrow cones of pale blue lightning. They streak upward from towering storm clouds in the troposphere below, moving at around 60 miles per second (100 kilometers per second)—300 times the speed of sound. They last just a fraction of a second.

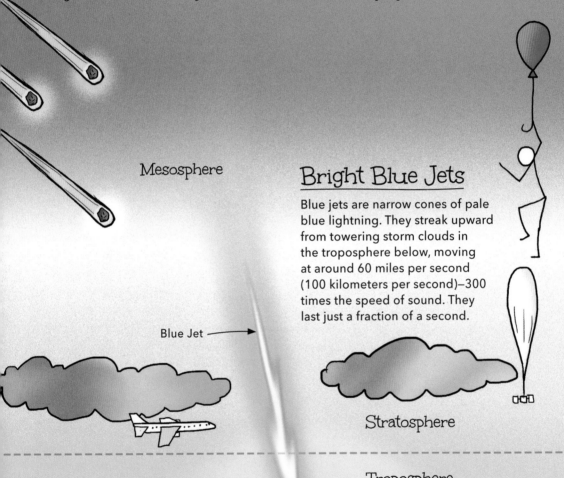

Blue Jet

Stratosphere

Troposphere

Storm Cloud

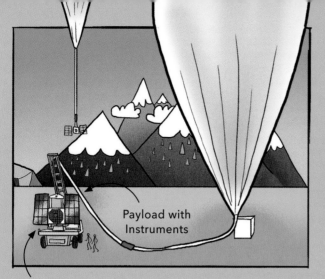

Payload with Instruments

Transporter

Studying Weather

Every day, hundreds of huge weather balloons, 6 feet (1.8 meters) in diameter, rise 20 miles (32 km) into the stratosphere. Each carries a radiosonde, which is a small bundle of instruments. They transmit data, such as temperature, pressure, wind speeds, and heat radiation levels to scientists, helping them to understand more about weather and climate.

Jetting High

Jet aircraft fly as much as possible in the lower part of the stratosphere, which is more stable than the stormy troposphere beneath it. The temperature in the stratosphere rises steadily and evenly with height, so hot and cold air mix less and there is less turbulence. Here, jet stream winds allow pilots to fly faster and save fuel.

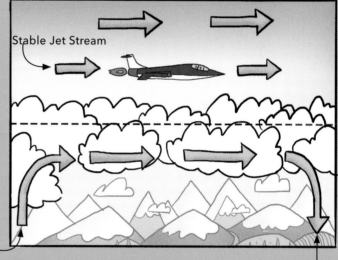

Stable Jet Stream

Warm, Moist Air

Rain or Snow

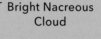
Bright Nacreous Cloud

Wavy Clouds

Mother-of-pearl or "nacreous" clouds in the stratosphere light up the evening sky with waves of rainbow colors, mostly at or toward the poles. They can be caused by winds much lower down, and occur at heights of around 13 miles (20 km). They are also known as winter Polar Stratospheric Clouds (PSCs).

The Ozone Layer

The protective ozone layer lies within the stratosphere around 10 to 24 miles (16 to 38 km) above Earth. Ozone is a type of oxygen molecule that can absorb the most harmful, burning UV light from the Sun, which prevents most of it from reaching the ground.

Burning Earth

A thinning ozone layer allows more of the Sun's damaging UV rays to get through. These rays burn our skin and prevent plant growth, and also contribute to coral bleaching (killing off coral reefs).

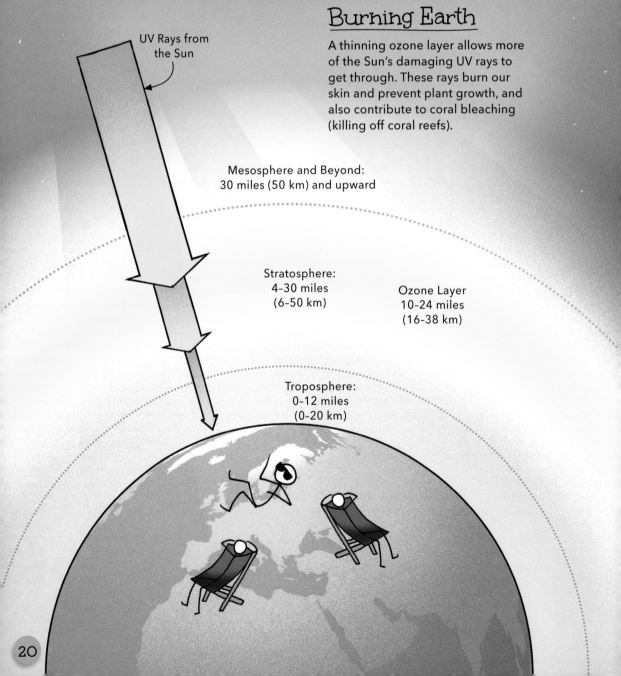

UV Rays from the Sun

Mesosphere and Beyond:
30 miles (50 km) and upward

Stratosphere:
4-30 miles
(6-50 km)

Ozone Layer
10-24 miles
(16-38 km)

Troposphere:
0-12 miles
(0-20 km)

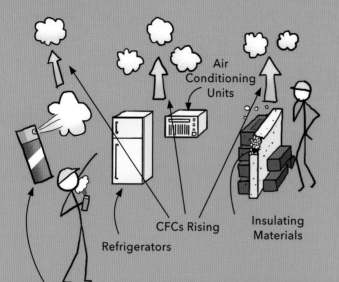

Damaging Gases

In the 1980s, it was found that when gases called cholorfluorocarbons (CFCs) were exposed to the Sun's strong UV light, they released chlorine into the atmosphere. This caused the ozone layer to become thinner. So CFCs, which were used in aerosols, air conditioning units, refrigerators, and insulating materials, were banned.

Air Conditioning Units

CFCs Rising

Insulating Materials

Refrigerators

Aerosols

Thinning Layer

The "hole" in the ozone layer is a region where the layer is thinner, especially over the poles in springtime. It was discovered in the Antarctic in 1984 by the British scientist Joseph Farman, who used a ground-level instrument called the Dobson spectrophotometer, or Dobsonmeter. Now, thermal images from space satellites track the size and shape of the hole.

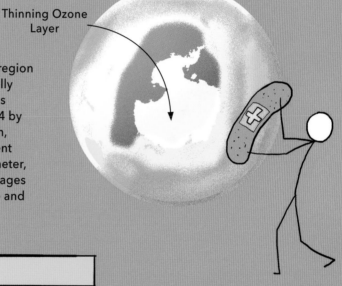

Thinning Ozone Layer

Dobsonmeter

Measuring the Ozone Layer

A Dobsonmeter works out how much ozone is absorbing the Sun's UV rays in the atmosphere. It was invented by the British meteorologist Gordon Dobson in the 1920s. Ozone levels in Antarctica reduce by about 50 percent in the worst years.

Earth's Troposphere

The troposphere is the layer that wraps immediately around Earth's surface. It reaches from sea level and varies in height up to 12 miles (20 km). It is the warmest layer, because Earth absorbs the Sun's warmth, then radiates it back up, heating the air near the ground.

The Air We Breathe

The troposphere is made up mainly of nitrogen with some oxygen and small amounts of other gases, including carbon dioxide. We need oxygen to breathe, and plants use carbon dioxide to grow.

Oxygen 21%

Nitrogen 78%

Other Gases 1%

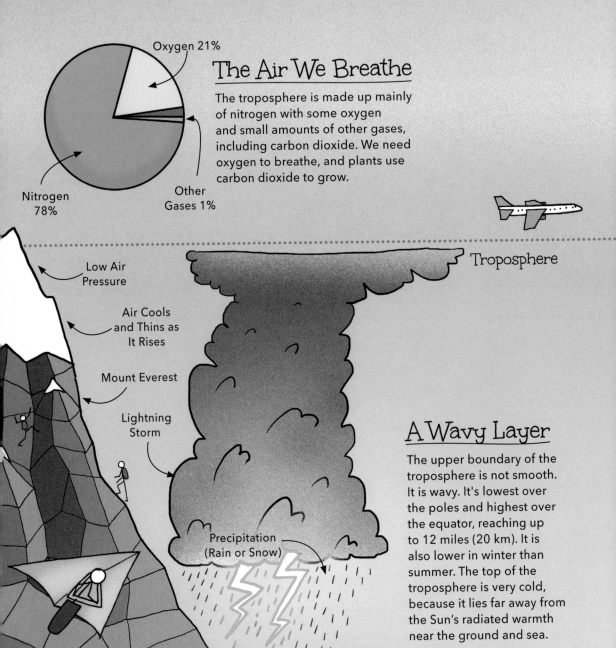

Troposphere

Low Air Pressure

Air Cools and Thins as It Rises

Mount Everest

Lightning Storm

Precipitation (Rain or Snow)

A Wavy Layer

The upper boundary of the troposphere is not smooth. It is wavy. It's lowest over the poles and highest over the equator, reaching up to 12 miles (20 km). It is also lower in winter than summer. The top of the troposphere is very cold, because it lies far away from the Sun's radiated warmth near the ground and sea.

Thinner on Top

Air gets thinner toward the top of the troposphere as air pressure drops. So there is less oxygen, which is why mountaineers usually carry oxygen supplies. This is also why airplane cabins are pressurized, providing the right oxygen levels and pressure for passengers and crew to breathe. Despite this, Rüppell's griffon vulture, one of the highest flying birds, has been recorded in flight at 37,000 feet (11,300 m)—even higher than an average commercial airplane.

Earth's Water Cycle

High in the troposphere, tall cloud columns rise. These form when the Sun heats up water from oceans and large lakes. The water evaporates from a liquid to a gas, which rises as it warms. High up, it cools and condenses into water droplets that form clouds. When the clouds are heavy with water, it falls as rain.

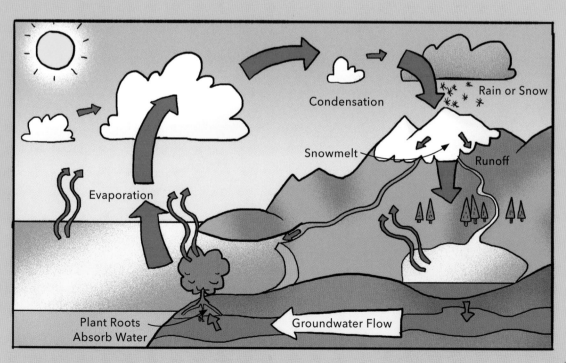

Condensation

Rain or Snow

Snowmelt

Runoff

Evaporation

Plant Roots
Absorb Water

Groundwater Flow

Storms and Twisters

Towering clouds in the troposphere bring strong winds, lashing rain, and snow blizzards. The most destructive storms are called hurricanes, cyclones, or typhoons, depending on where they blow. Twisting tornadoes suck up all that lies in their path.

Satellite

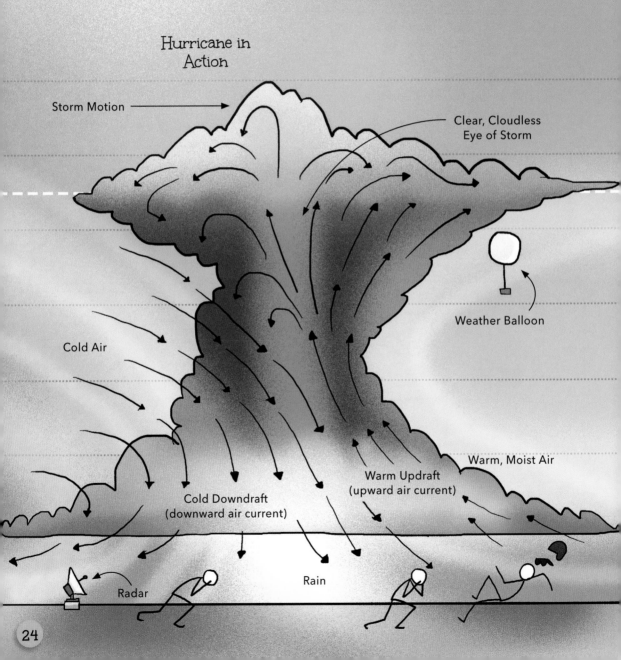

Hurricane in Action

Storm Motion

Clear, Cloudless Eye of Storm

Weather Balloon

Cold Air

Warm, Moist Air

Cold Downdraft
(downward air current)

Warm Updraft
(upward air current)

Radar

Rain

Hurricanes from Space

Satellites track the paths of hurricanes, which are wide banks of storm clouds rotating around a calm center (called the "eye"). Hurricanes develop over warm oceans, where winds pick up huge amounts of moist air. The moisture rises and forms clouds that are swirled around by driving winds. Hurricanes smack the land with destructive force and push up enormous waves, causing serious flooding.

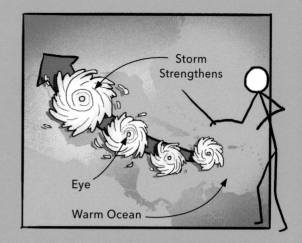

Storm Strengthens

Eye

Warm Ocean

Making Rain

Climate change is making some regions on Earth drier. In some dry zones, rain clouds are artificially created. This is done by "seeding" the air with chemicals. They draw together water droplets in the air to form clouds. The chemicals can be spread by aircraft or released by rockets and other launching equipment from the ground.

Seed-clouding Machine

Twister!

Tornadoes blow along land, picking up warm moisture that rises until it hits very cold air at the top. This condenses it into tall, dark storm clouds. The clouds are blown by high-up winds from different directions, turning them into twisting, sucking storms that touch down in a funnel shape. Tornadoes can pick up houses, or even drop showers of frogs far away!

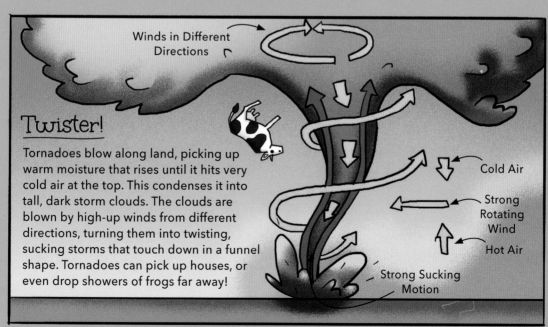

Winds in Different Directions

Cold Air

Strong Rotating Wind

Hot Air

Strong Sucking Motion

What's the Weather Like?

Weather encompasses the heat and cold, rain, snow, fog, and wind that affect us every day on Earth. Observers at weather stations monitor temperature, humidity, wind speed, and direction, and rain or snowfall on a daily and hourly basis. Their data is vital for making weather forecasts, ensuring people's safety, and studying climate change.

What a Wind!

Wind speeds can tell us how quickly a weather system, such as a storm, will reach us. They are measured with an anemometer, which captures the wind in rotating cups connected to an electric generator. This creates an electric current, which can be measured. A strong wind makes a high current.

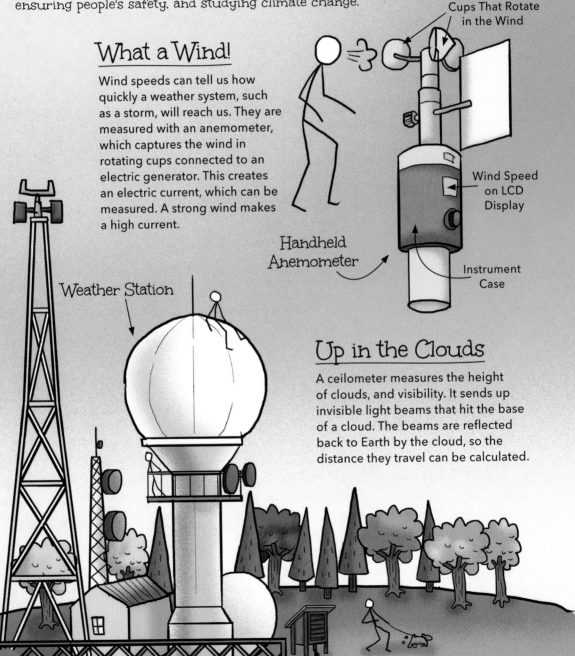

Cups That Rotate in the Wind

Wind Speed on LCD Display

Handheld Anemometer

Instrument Case

Weather Station

Up in the Clouds

A ceilometer measures the height of clouds, and visibility. It sends up invisible light beams that hit the base of a cloud. The beams are reflected back to Earth by the cloud, so the distance they travel can be calculated.

Ceilometer

How Hot Is It?

The first true thermometer for measuring temperature accurately was invented in 1724 by German physicist Gabriel Fahrenheit. He set a column of mercury, enclosed in glass, against a scale of measurement. Alcohol is now used instead of mercury, which is dangerous, while digital thermometers (right) are the latest technology. These may have a wireless sensor for use at a distance from the main unit. We still use degrees Fahrenheit as a temperature scale.

Indoor 64.9 °F

Outdoor 75.2 °F

8:04

Digital Thermometer

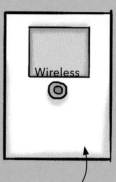

Wireless

Wireless Sensor (for relaying temperature data to the receiver unit)

Under Pressure

Air pressure is the pressure exerted by the weight of air pushing down on Earth from above. It tells us roughly the type of weather we can expect for a few days. High air pressure usually brings clear skies and sunshine; low air pressure means rain or a storm! Barometers measure air pressure.

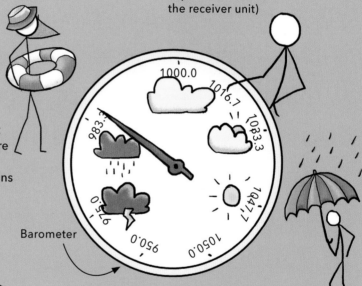

1000.0
1016.7
1033.3
983.3
1047.7
976.0
950.0
1050.0

Barometer

Hygrometer

Moderate

40 50

Dry 30 60

20 70

10 80 Moist

0 90

100

%

Measuring Humidity

We use a hygrometer to measure the air's moisture, or humidity. It tells us how much water vapor is in the air, and when it will form water droplets. This is important in such processes as applying paint and in conserving artworks and musical instruments.

Fantastic Atmosphere Facts

Blue Moon

A truly blue Moon is a very rare sight. It only appears when huge amounts of smoke or dust particles are thrust high into the atmosphere, usually from volcanoes, allowing only blue light waves through. After the devastating eruption of the volcanic island of Krakatau in Indonesia in 1883, the Moon looked blue for months!

Crash!

More and more satellites are being launched into space. Over time, their orbits gradually change, so there is a risk of satellites crashing into each other. In 2009, two communication satellites collided for the first time. One was Russian and the other American, and both were destroyed.

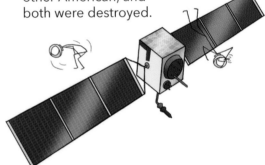

Fast Food Delivery

How do astronauts on the ISS survive? Unmanned spacecraft called Automated Transfer Vehicles (ATVs) deliver fuel, food, and science equipment. Scientists on Earth send a wide variety of foods to the astronauts. This is so they can study the effect of each food on humans in weightless space.

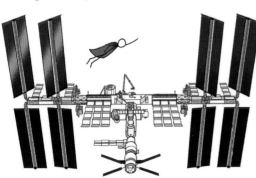

Is There Life Out There?

The Hubble Space Telescope has been used to study the atmospheres of exoplanets—planets that orbit around other stars. About two thousand exoplanets have been discovered and there could be billions of Earth-like planets in our Milky Way galaxy. But do they have life?

Fragile Ozone Layer

The ozone layer reacts quickly and strongly to extra chlorine gases. Just one chlorine atom can destroy more than one hundred thousand ozone molecules. Many extra chlorine and other harmful gases in the ozone layer are man-made. When they meet with high-rising gases from erupting volcanoes, they increase the damaging effect on the ozone layer.

Poisonous Ozone!

Ten percent of all ozone is below the stratosphere. Here, ozone does not protect Earth from UV rays. Instead, it pollutes the air we breathe and can cause health problems. It also enters plant and crop systems, damaging growth. This ozone derives from industrial chemicals released into the air.

The Worst Hurricanes

Off the coast of Mexico in 2015, Hurricane Patricia's wind speed reached 200 miles per hour (325 km/h), and it was declared the worst hurricane in history. Fortunately, there was no loss of life. On the other side of the Pacific in 2013, Typhoon Haiyan reached a wind speed of 195 miles per hour (315 km/h). It hit the Philippines, killing 6,300 people. So the impact of a hurricane does not depend on wind speed alone.

Most Terrible Tornado

The worst tornado registered so far touched down on March 18 ,1925. It twisted 300 miles (480 km) through Missouri, Illinois, and Indiana—three states in what is known as Tornado Alley. It reached at least 260 miles per hour (415 km/h), and 695 people died, with more than two thousand injured. Buildings were reduced to sticks and stones.

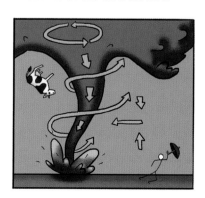

The Future...

The atmosphere's layers hold vital clues to the causes of climate change, as the Earth becomes warmer and sea levels rise. Studying our atmosphere has given scientists the tools to find out if we can survive on other planets...

Studying Climate Change

The rate of Earth's temperature rise has doubled in the last fifty years. Is there a single cause, or several working together? Scientists study the gas types and movements in all Earth's layers to find out. They monitor greenhouse gases: carbon dioxide, methane, and nitrous oxide, which hold in the Sun's heat as it radiates from Earth. The results, together with thermal images from satellites and computer modeling, help us understand the future of our climate.

Other Factors

The Sun's flares and sunspots may also be contributing to climate change. Scientists follow the Sun's effects on our planet, as Earth's distance from the Sun changes over a year and activity on the Sun varies. They are also looking in greater detail at the sources of pollution in our atmosphere. Small robotic drones hover over waste dumps to measure how much methane, a toxic gas, is rising skyward!

Life on Mars?

Since 2004, mobile robots called rovers have been used on Mars to find out if the conditions there could ever have sustained life. The samples taken confirm that the atmosphere on Mars is now very thin, and that 95.3 percent of it consists of carbon dioxide. Since 2012, the Rover *Curiosity* has sent results proving that Mars once had surface water—one of the essential ingredients for life to exist.

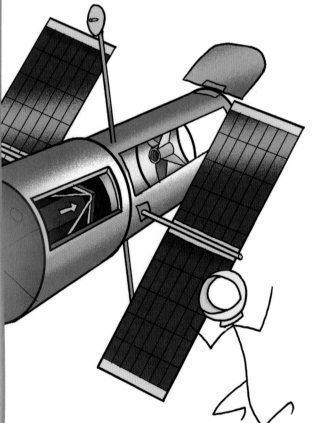

Glossary

comet:
small solar system object that grows tails of dust and gas when it gets near the Sun

cyclone:
powerful rotating storm system

galaxy:
large system of stars, dust, and gas held together by gravity

gravity:
the force that pulls objects toward Earth's surface and each other

hypersonic:
speeds above five times the speed of sound

infrared:
radiation with longer wavelengths than visible light

meteor:
small rock or other matter from space that enters Earth's atmosphere, burning as a streak of light in the sky

orbit:
path followed by one body in space around another, such as a satellite around Earth

radiation:
a form of energy that can travel through empty space, such as light or X-rays

pressurized:
having a gas pressure inside that is greater than the pressure outside

sounding rocket:
a rocket carrying instruments that collect data or carry out experiments in space

ultraviolet:
invisible radiation similar to light, but more powerful and with shorter wavelengths

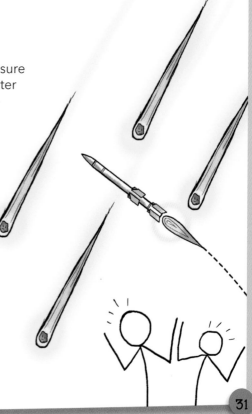

INDEX

The Author

Catherine Chambers was born in Adelaide, South Australia, grew up in the United Kingdom and studied African History and Swahili at the School of Oriental and African Studies in London. She has written about 130 books for children and young adults, and enjoys seeking out intriguing facts for her nonfiction titles, which cover history, cultures, faiths, biography, geography, and the environment.

The Illustrator

John Paul has a BSc in Biology from the University of Sussex, United Kingdom, and a graduate certificate in animation from the University of the West of England. He devotes his spare time to growing chili peppers, perfecting his plan for a sustainable future, and caring for a small plastic dinosaur. He has three pet squid that live in the bath, which makes drawing in ink quite economical . . .

Picture Credits (abbreviations: t = top; b = bottom; c = center; l = left; r = right)
15 tr NASA, ESA, and the Hubble Heritage Team (STScI/AURA)